Meditative Mandala Coloring Pages

Volume 1

Meditative Mandala Coloring Pages Vol. 1
by Kipling Creative

© 2023 Kipling Creative. All rights reserved.
Printed in the United States of America.

Published by Kipling Creative, Houston, Texas.

No part of this publication may be reproduced, stored in a retrieval system or transmited in any form or by any means, electronic, mechanical, photocopying, recording or otherwise without the prior permision of the publisher or in accordance with the provisions of the Copyright, Designs and Patents Act 1988 or under the terms of any licence permitting limited copying issued by the Copyright Licensing Angency.

ISBN-13: 9

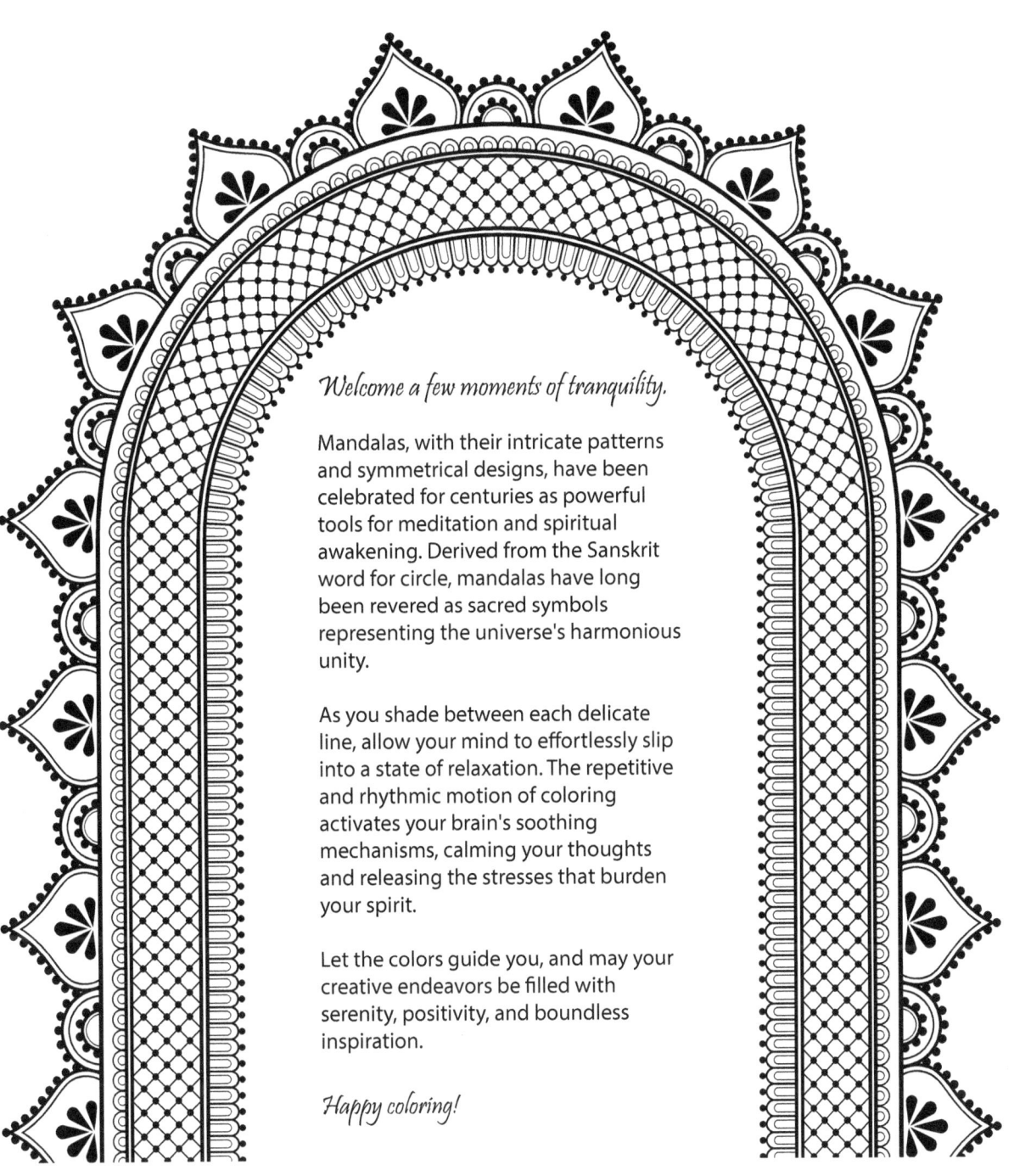

Welcome a few moments of tranquility.

Mandalas, with their intricate patterns and symmetrical designs, have been celebrated for centuries as powerful tools for meditation and spiritual awakening. Derived from the Sanskrit word for circle, mandalas have long been revered as sacred symbols representing the universe's harmonious unity.

As you shade between each delicate line, allow your mind to effortlessly slip into a state of relaxation. The repetitive and rhythmic motion of coloring activates your brain's soothing mechanisms, calming your thoughts and releasing the stresses that burden your spirit.

Let the colors guide you, and may your creative endeavors be filled with serenity, positivity, and boundless inspiration.

Happy coloring!

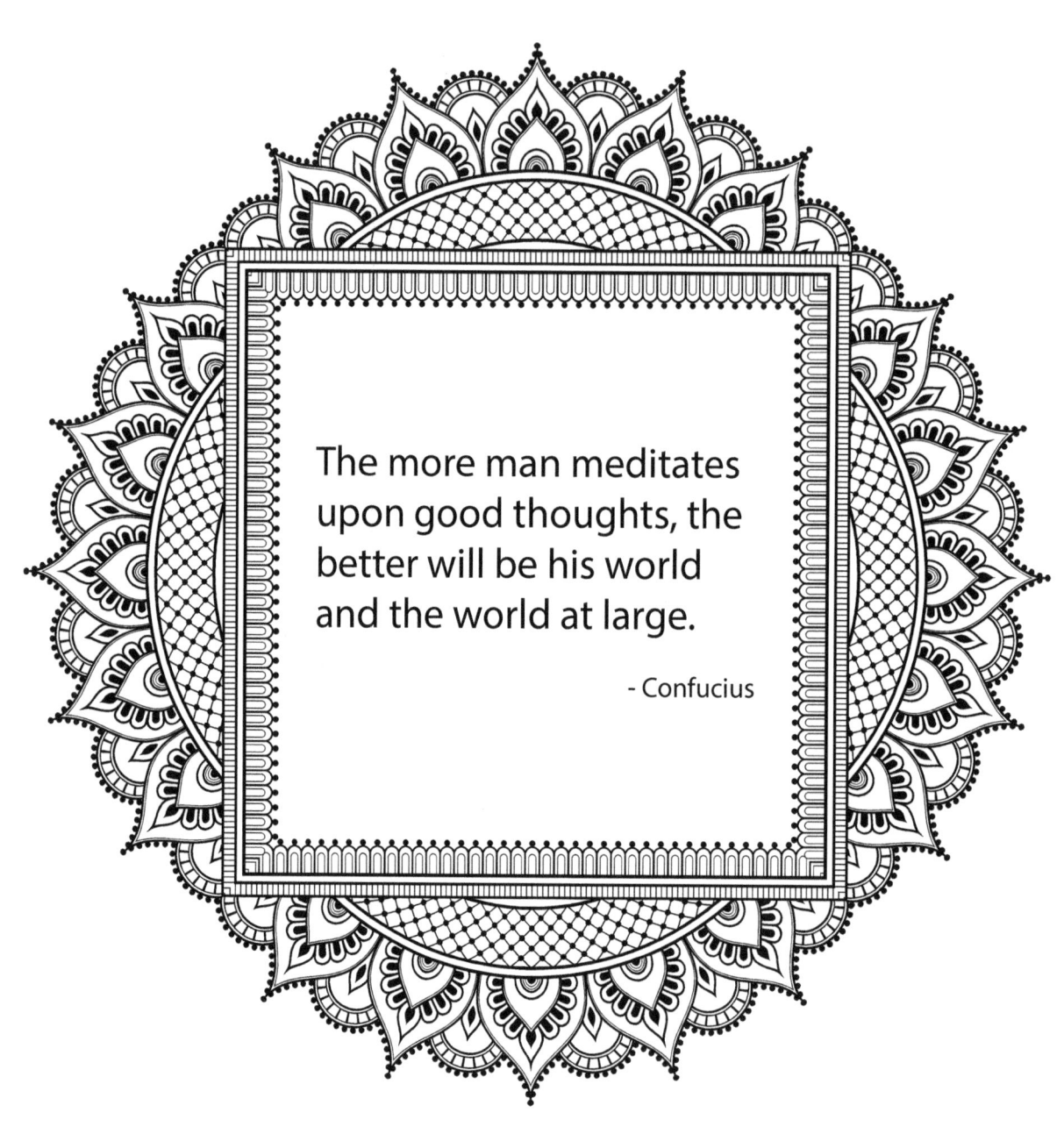

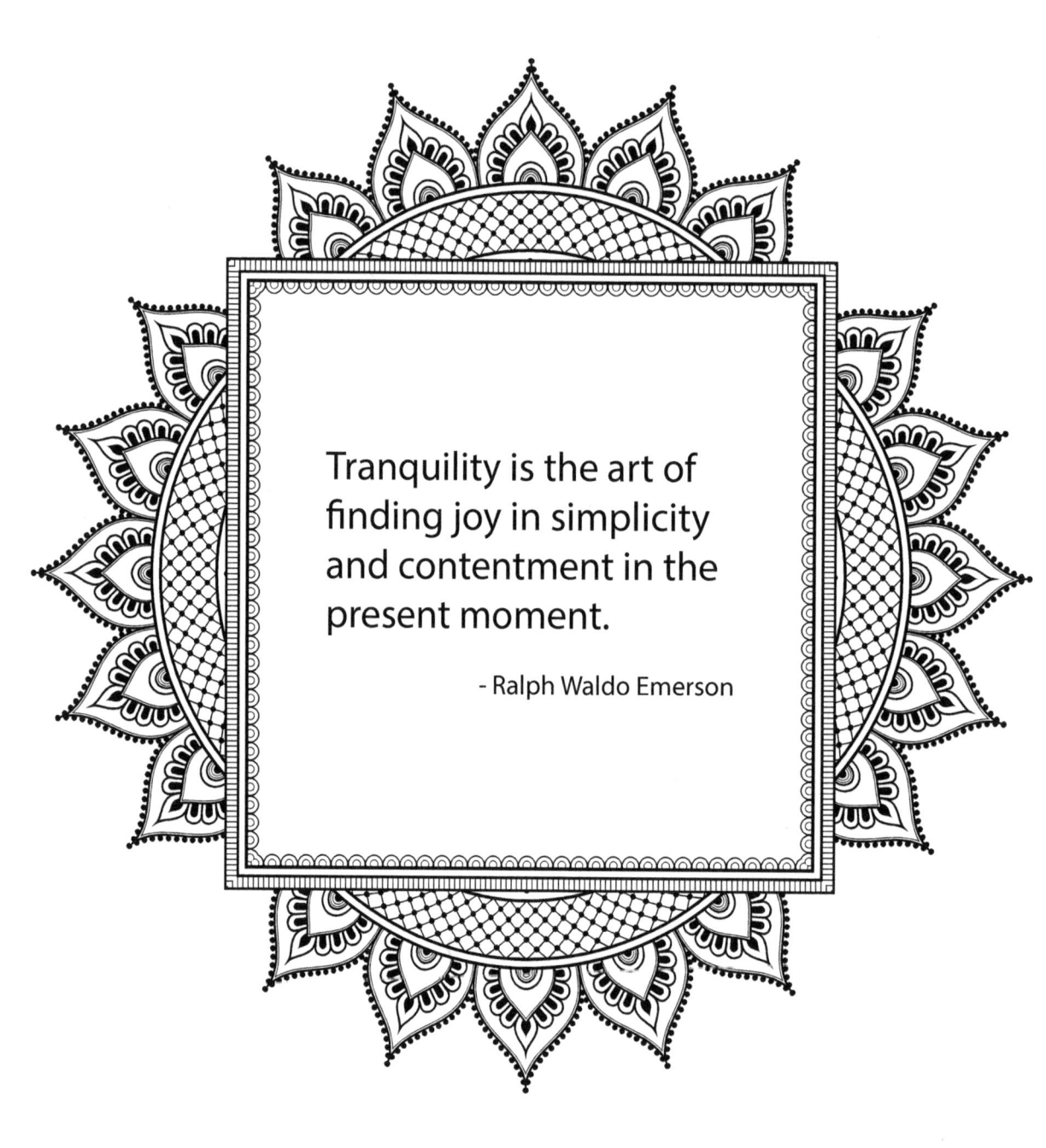

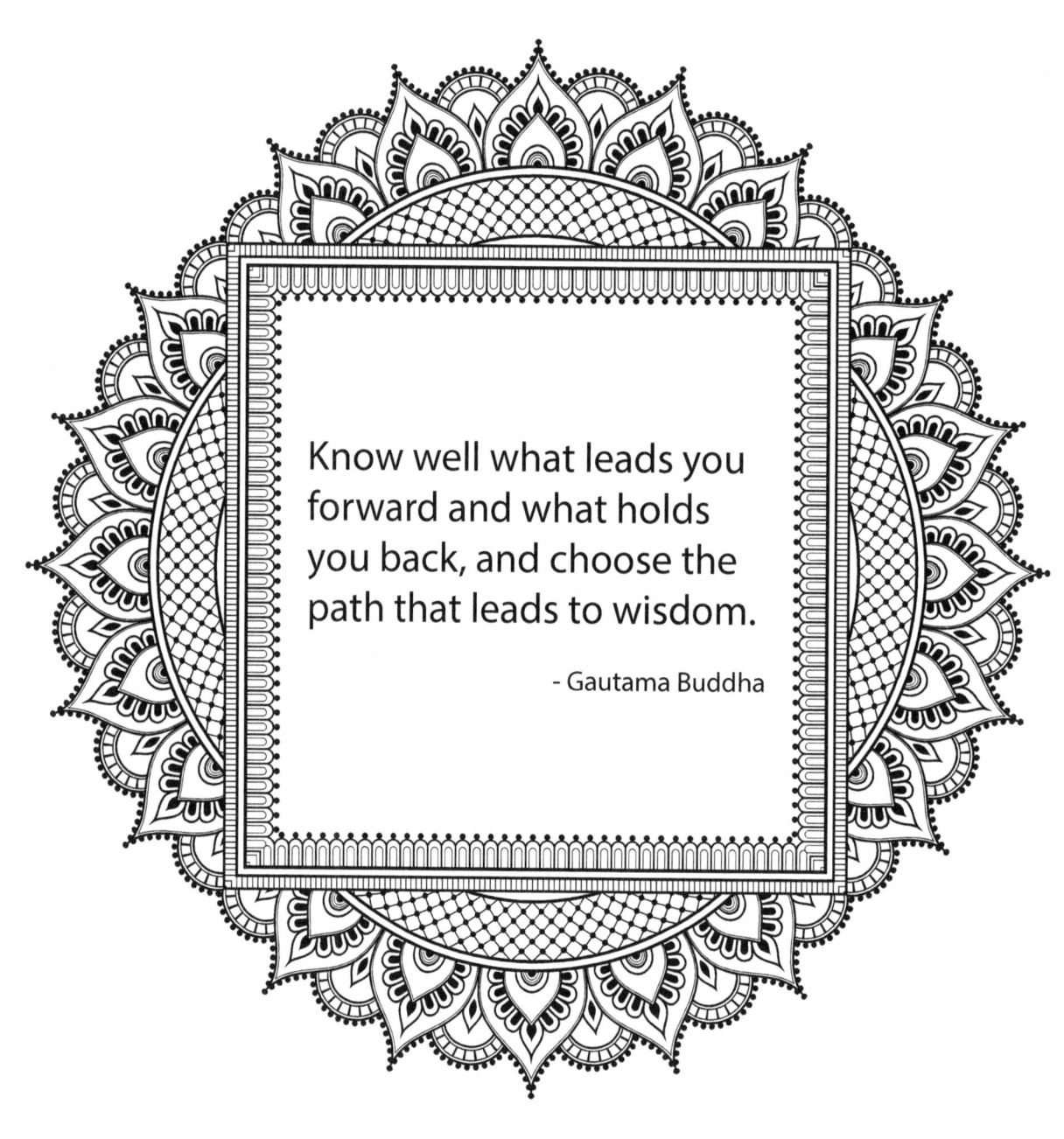

Know well what leads you forward and what holds you back, and choose the path that leads to wisdom.

- Gautama Buddha

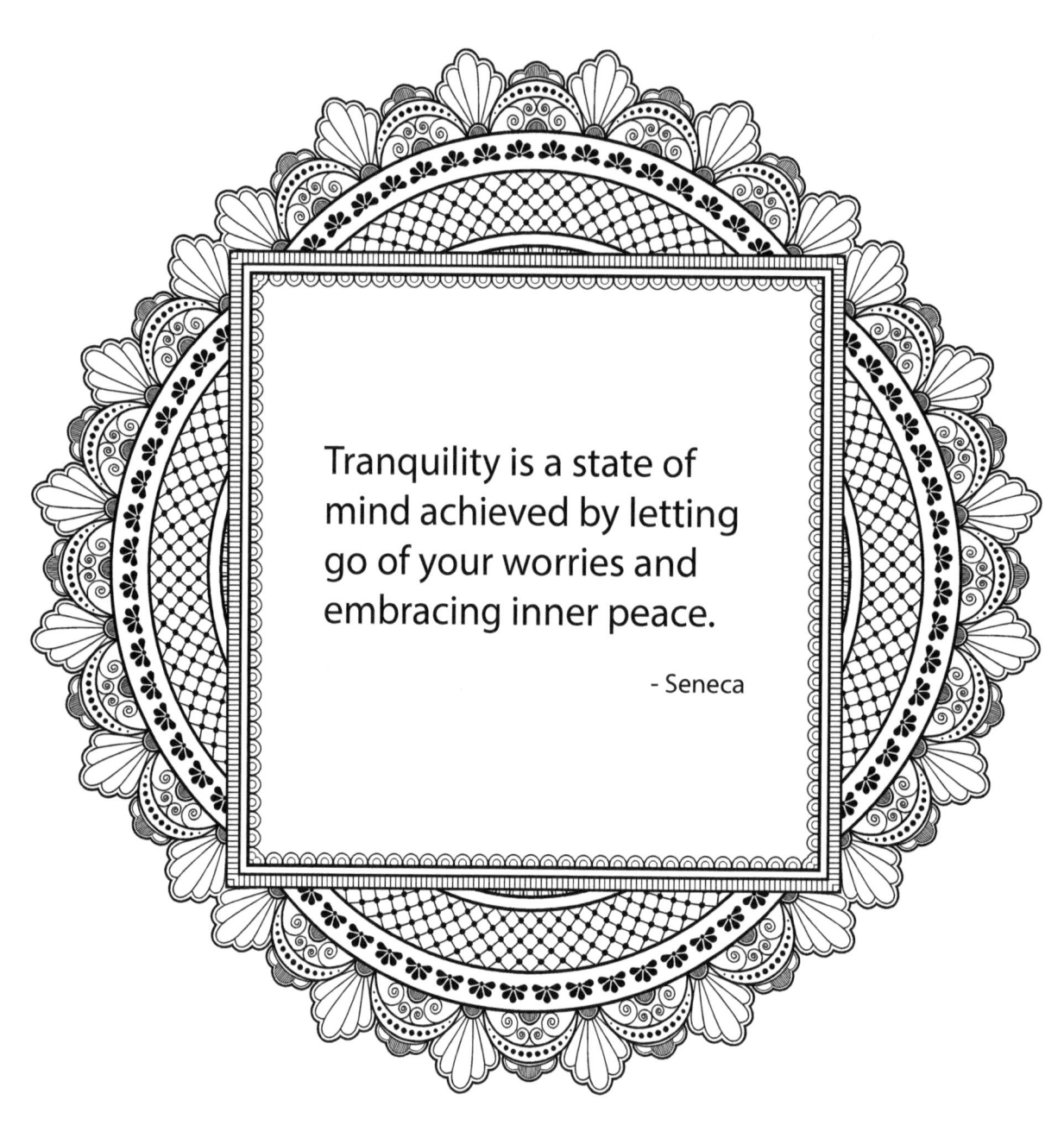

Tranquility is a state of mind achieved by letting go of your worries and embracing inner peace.

- Seneca

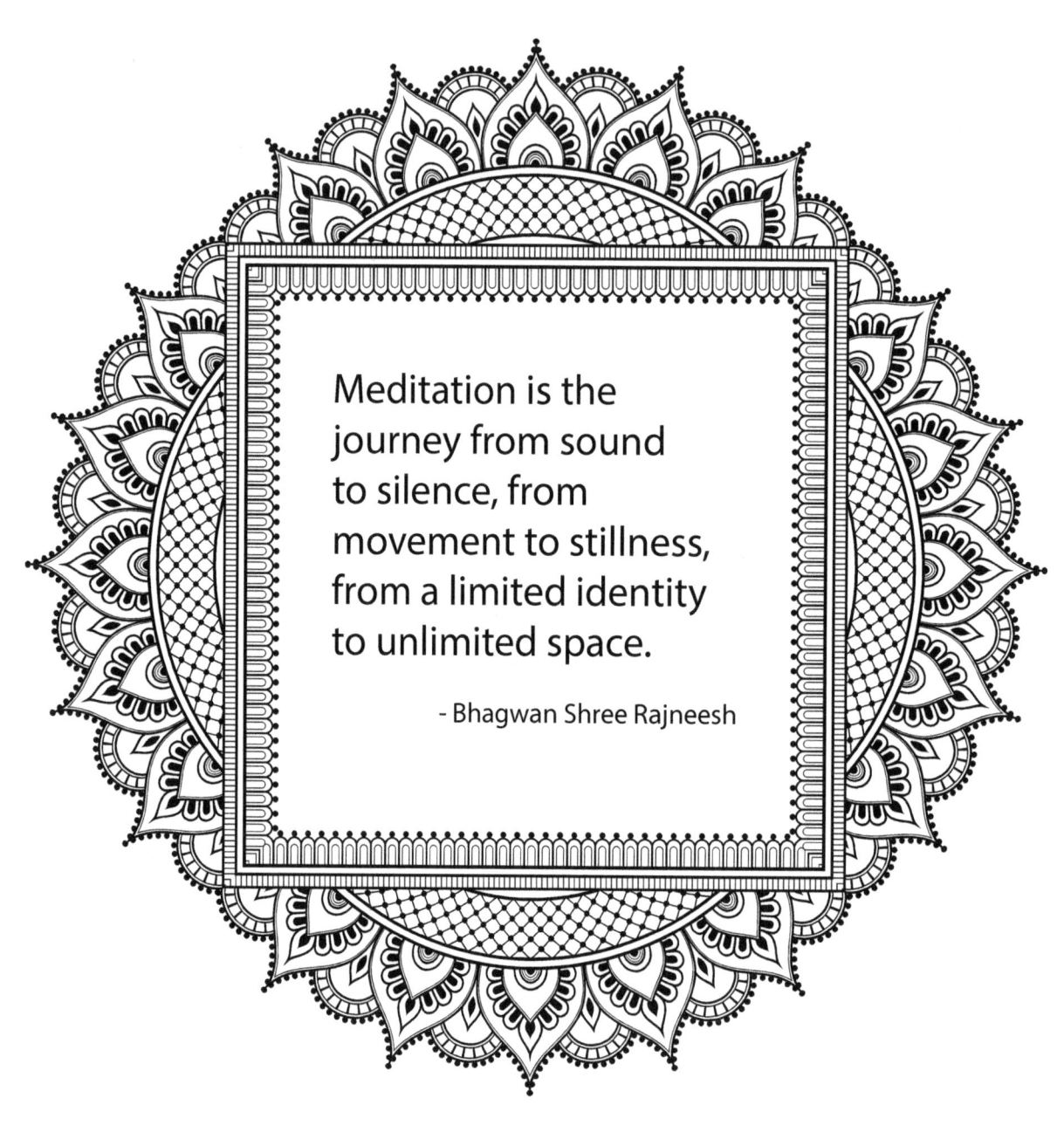

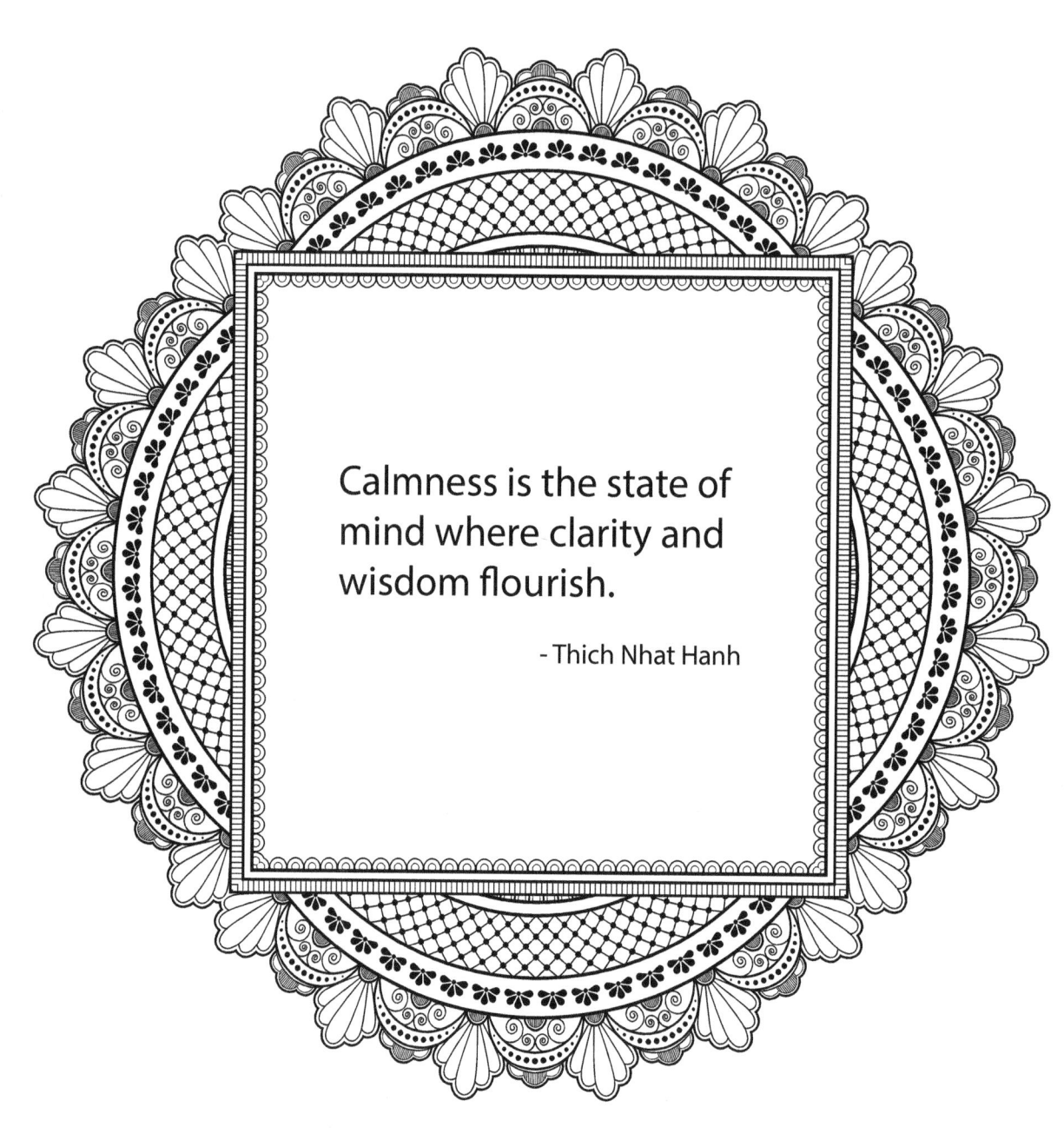

Calmness is the state of mind where clarity and wisdom flourish.

- Thich Nhat Hanh

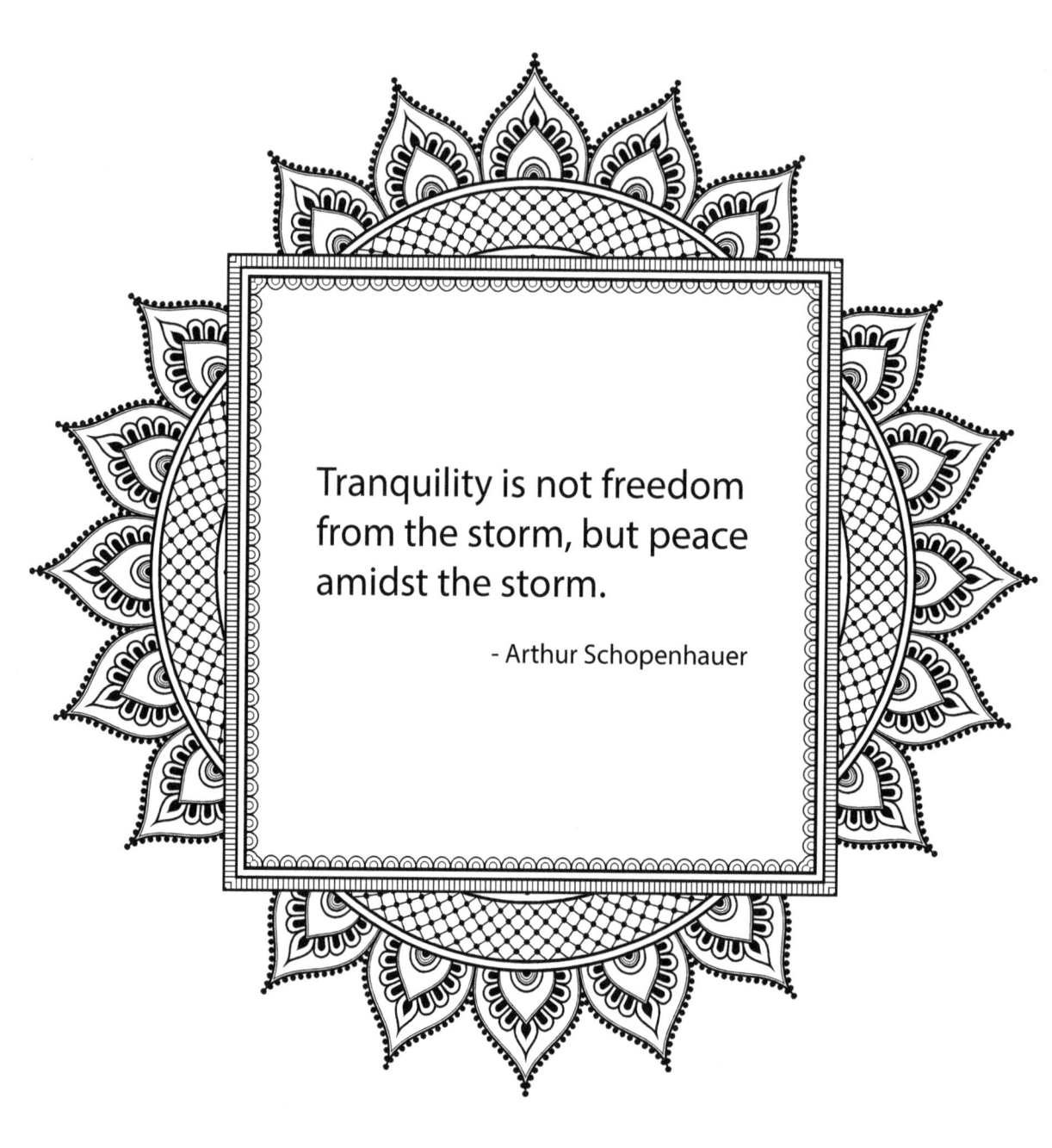

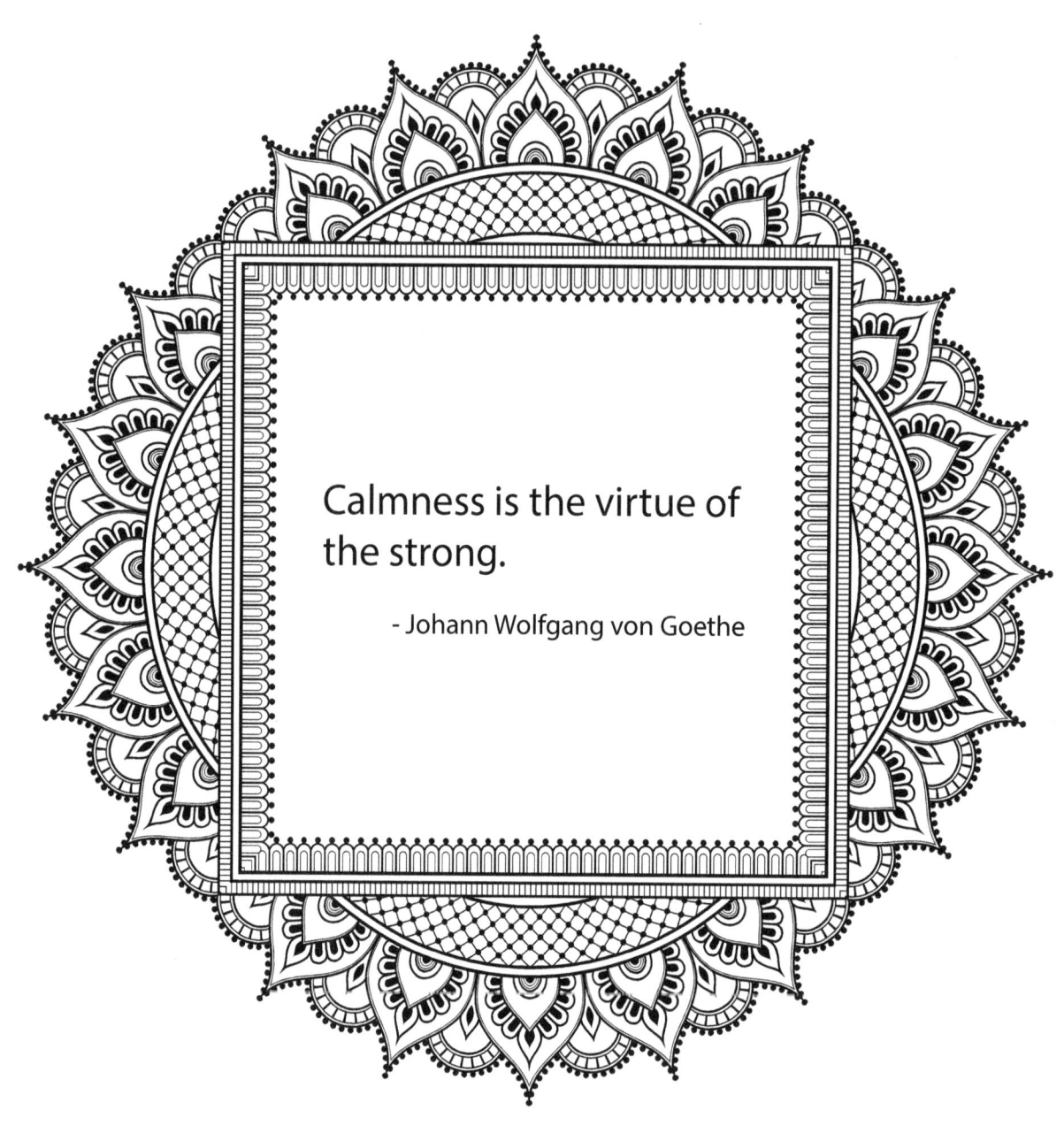

Calmness is the virtue of the strong.

- Johann Wolfgang von Goethe

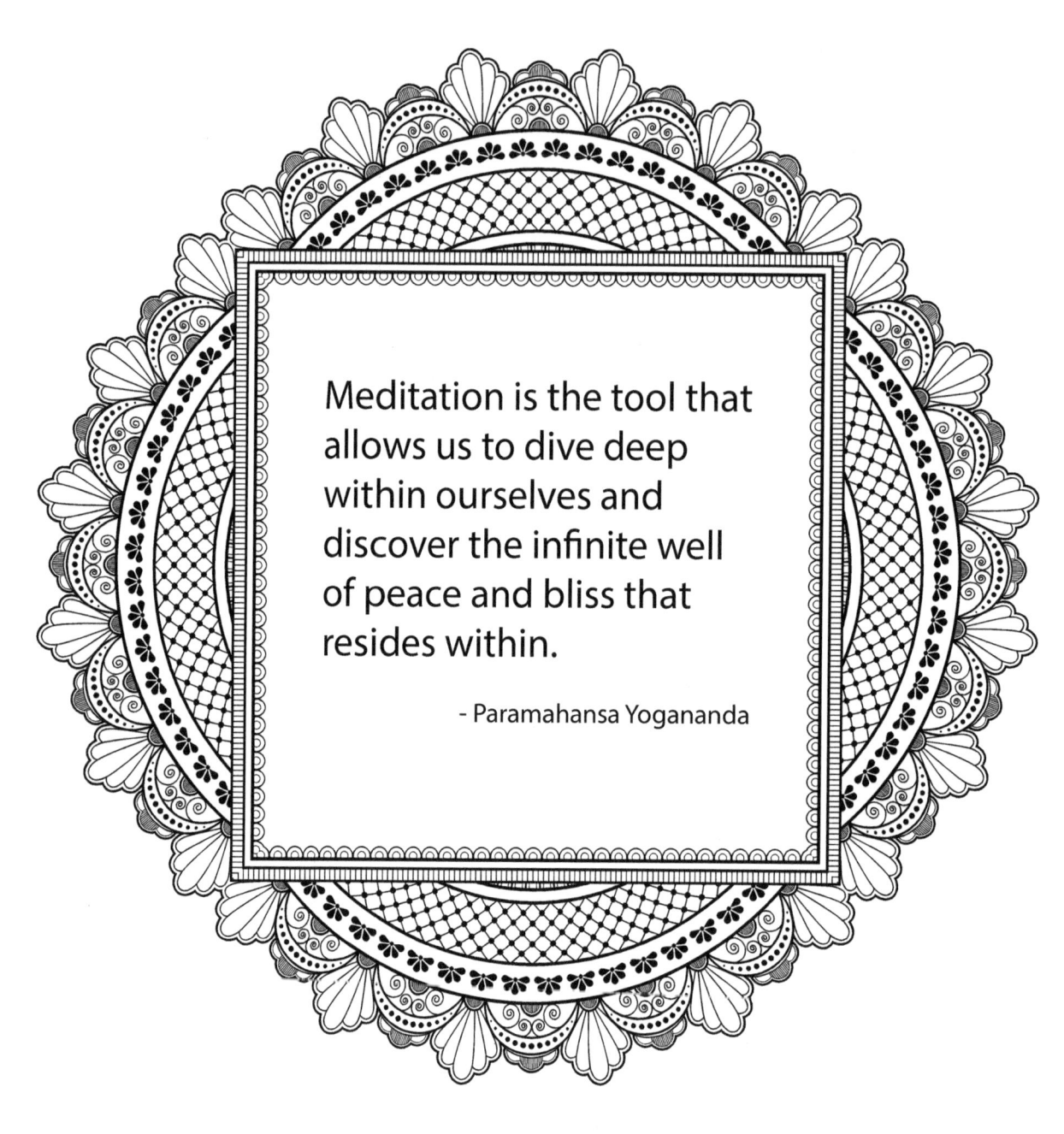

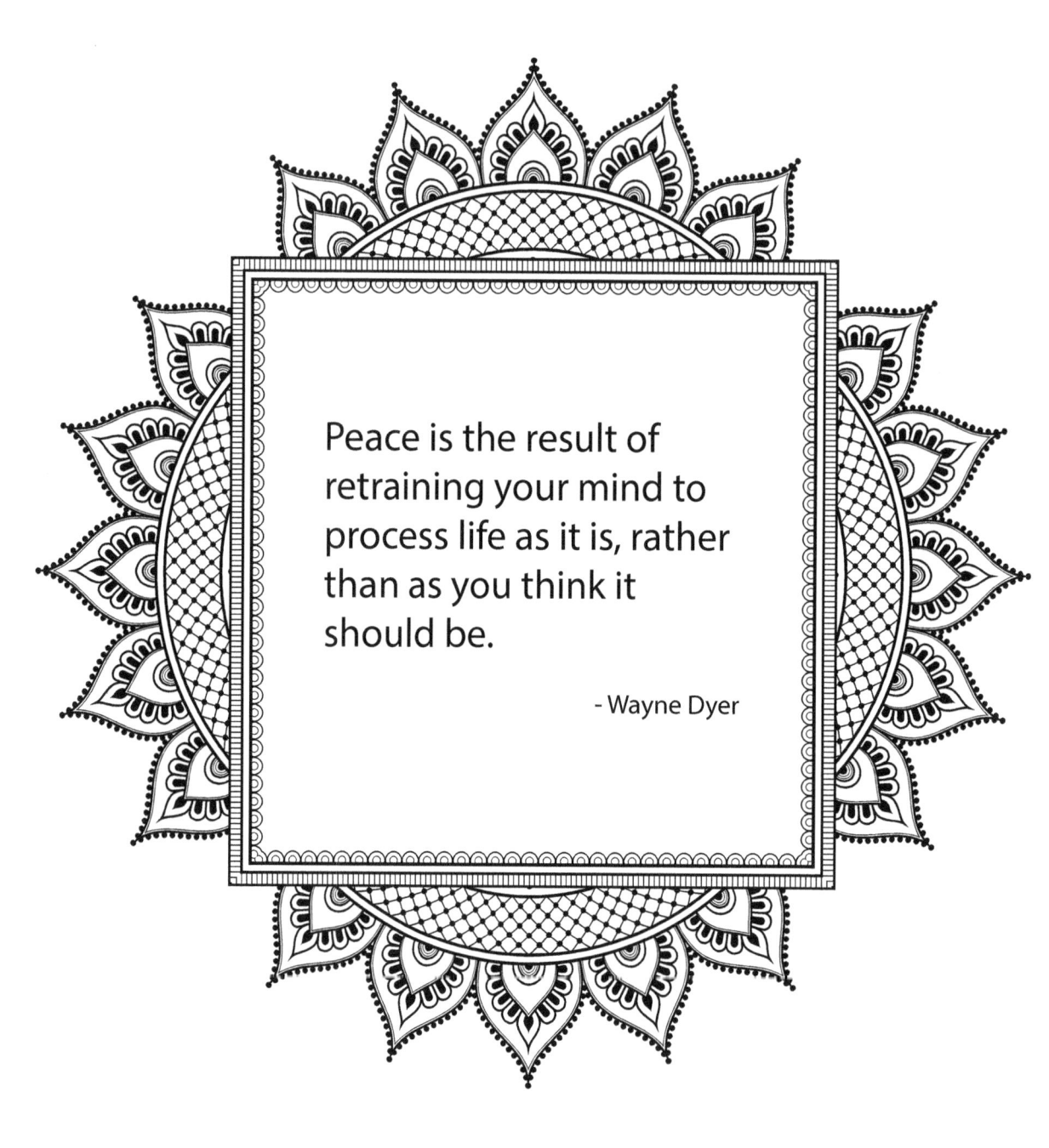

Peace is the result of retraining your mind to process life as it is, rather than as you think it should be.

- Wayne Dyer

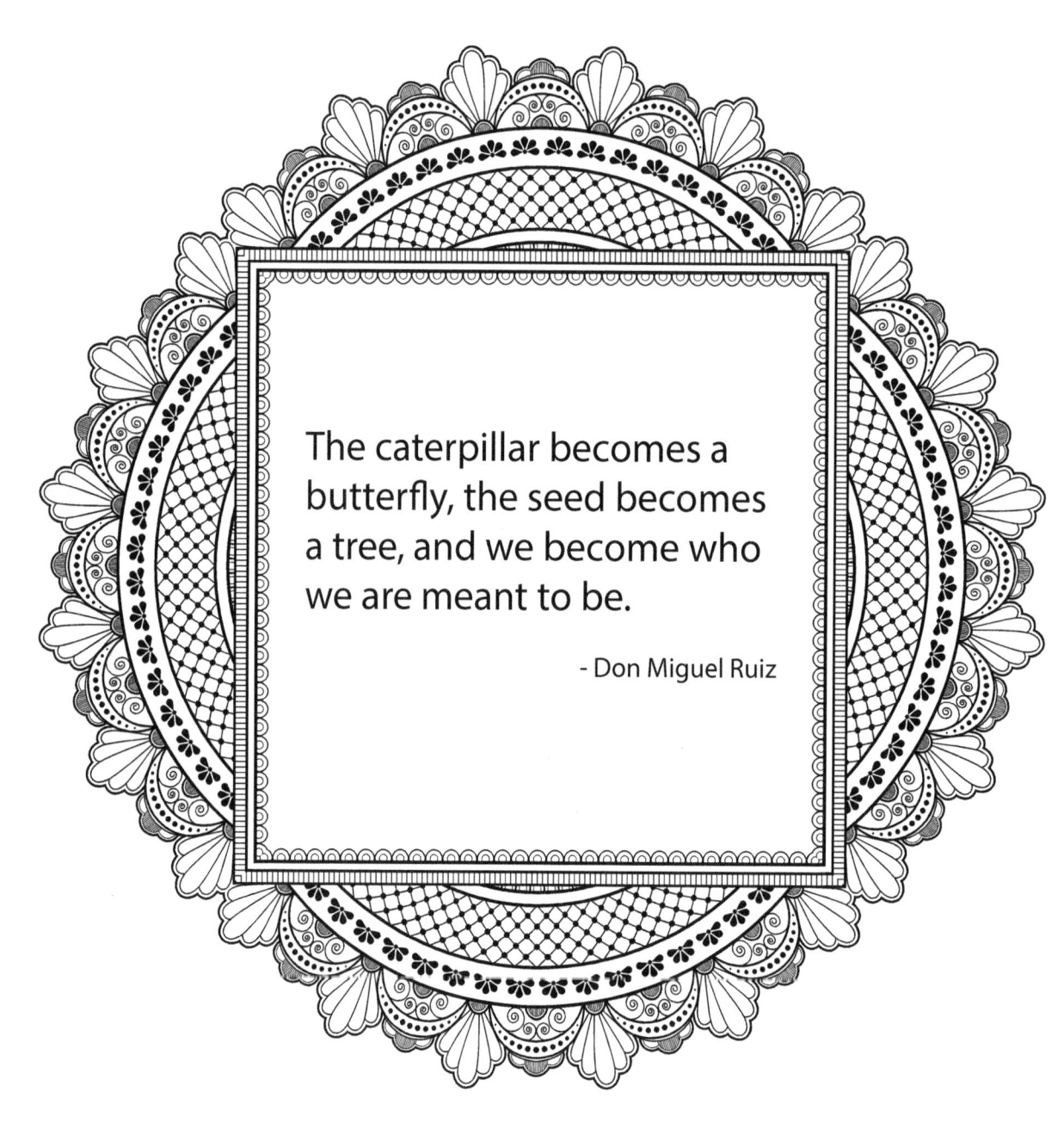

The caterpillar becomes a butterfly, the seed becomes a tree, and we become who we are meant to be.

- Don Miguel Ruiz

Transformation is not a future event, but a present activity.

- Eckhart Tolle

The good life is one that is rich in experiences, relationships, and gratitude.

- Seneca

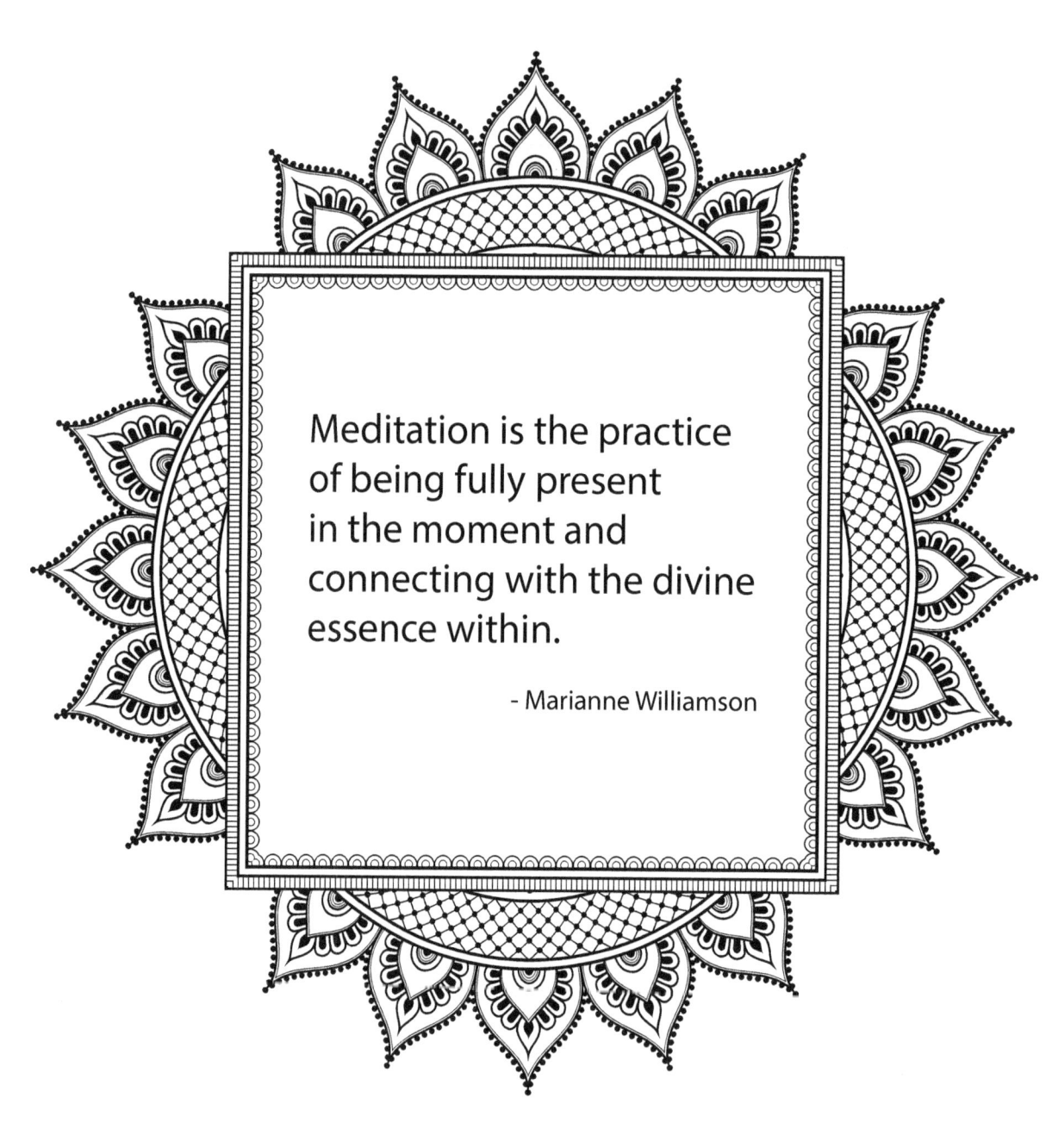

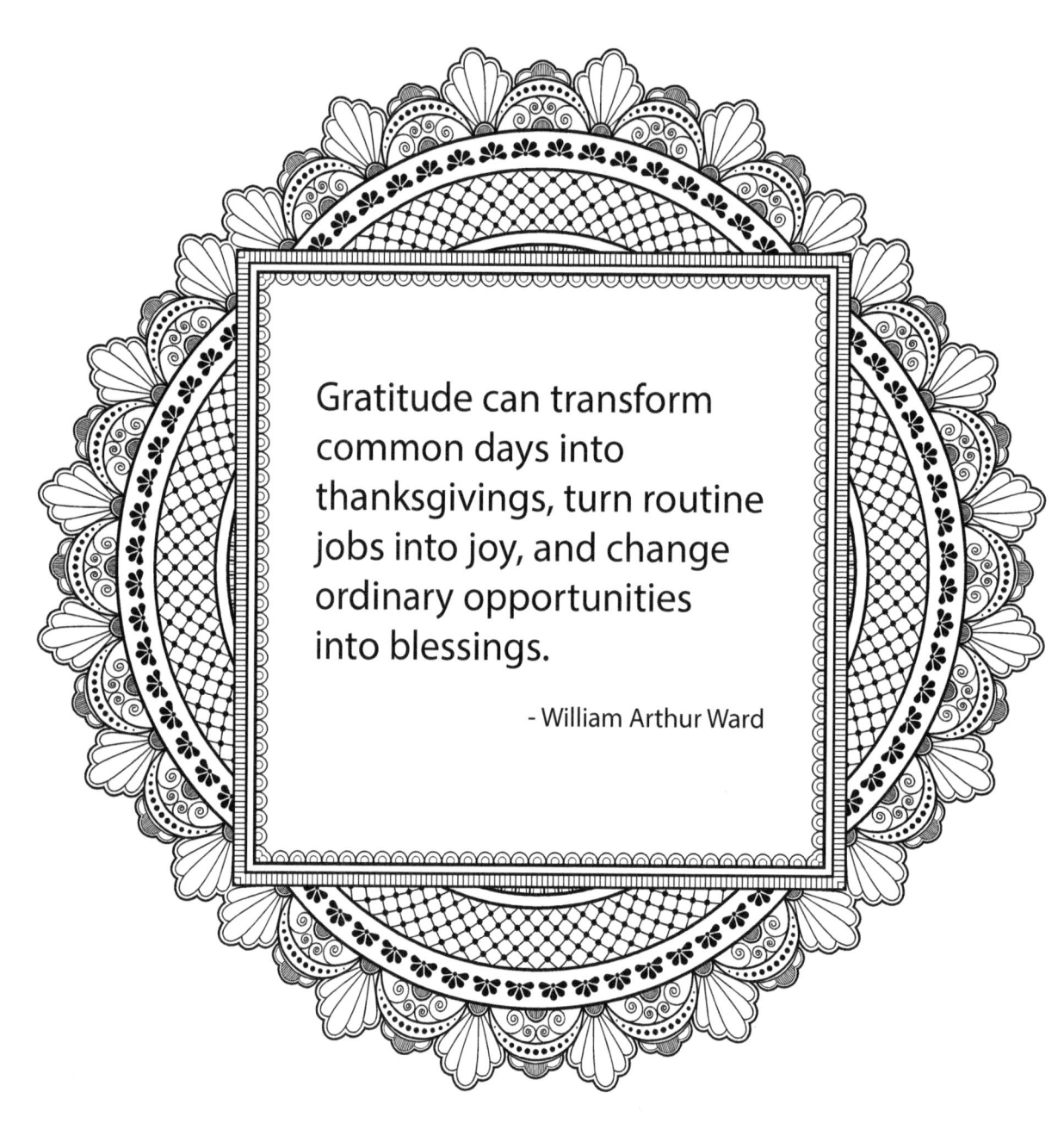

Gratitude can transform common days into thanksgivings, turn routine jobs into joy, and change ordinary opportunities into blessings.

- William Arthur Ward

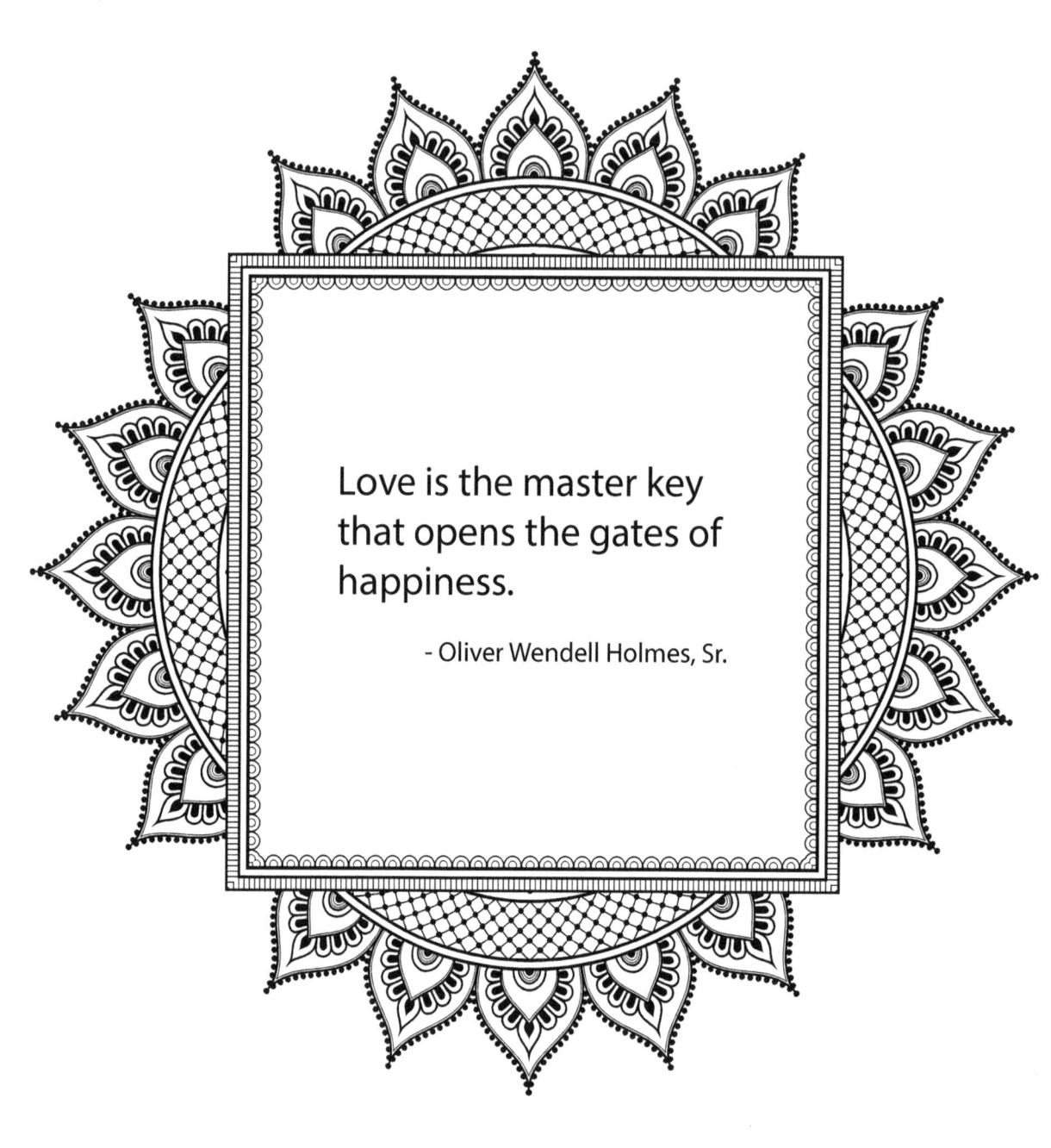

Love is the master key that opens the gates of happiness.

- Oliver Wendell Holmes, Sr.

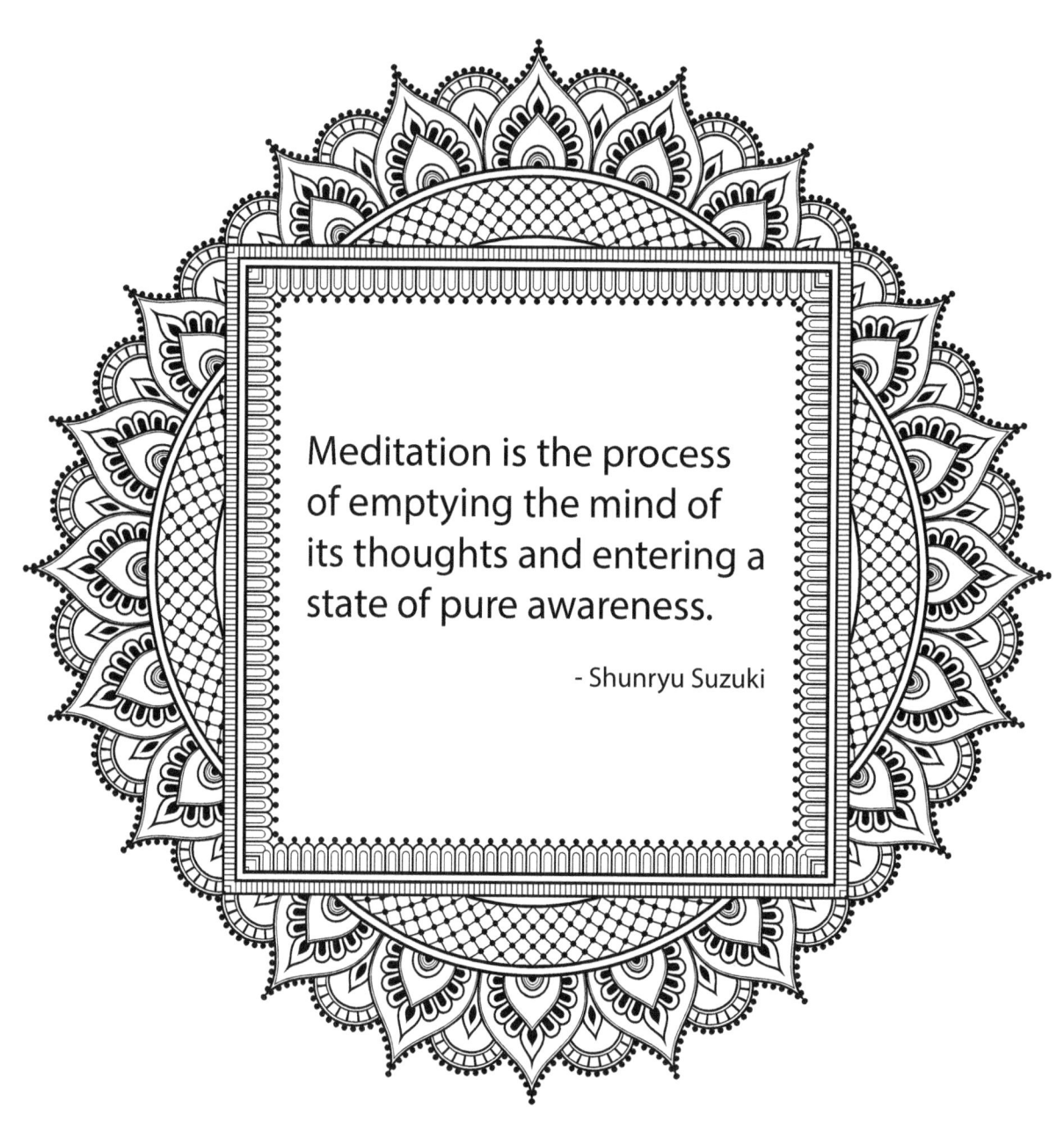

Transformation is the willingness to let go of who you have been in order to become who you are meant to be.

- Brené Brown

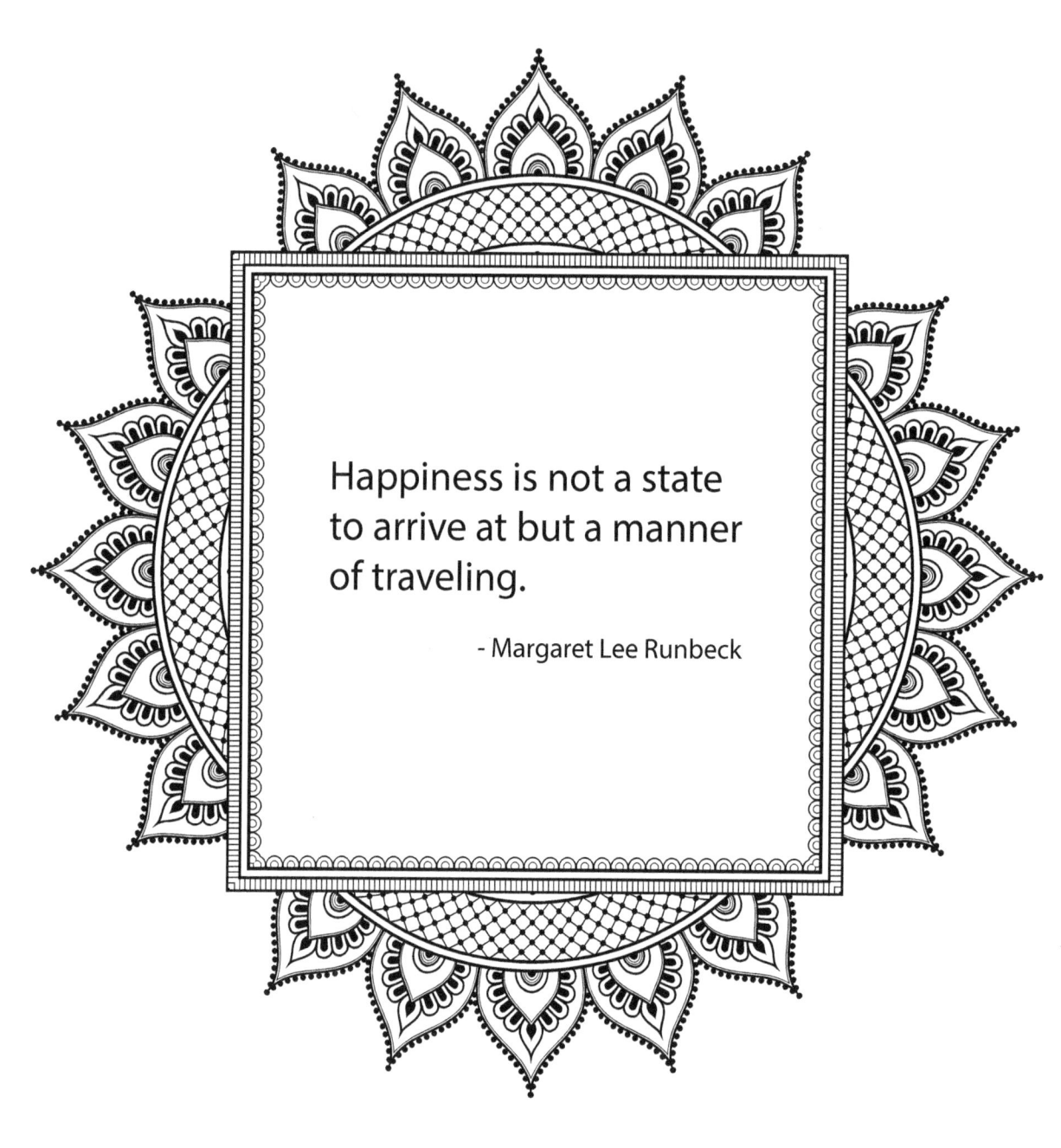

Love is a friendship
set to music.

- Joseph Campbell

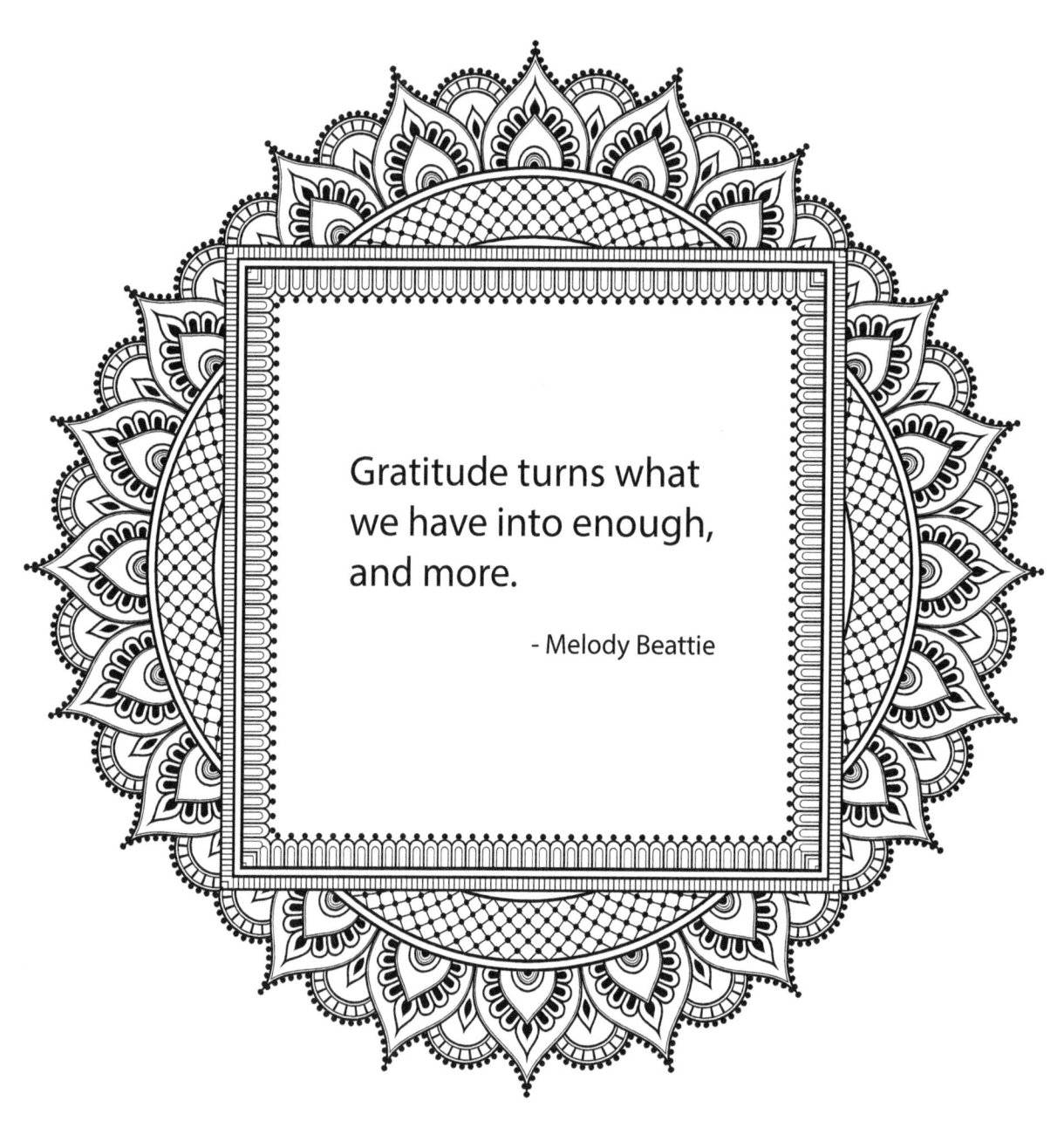

Transformation is not a sudden, spontaneous event. It is a gradual process that unfolds over time.

- Paulo Coelho

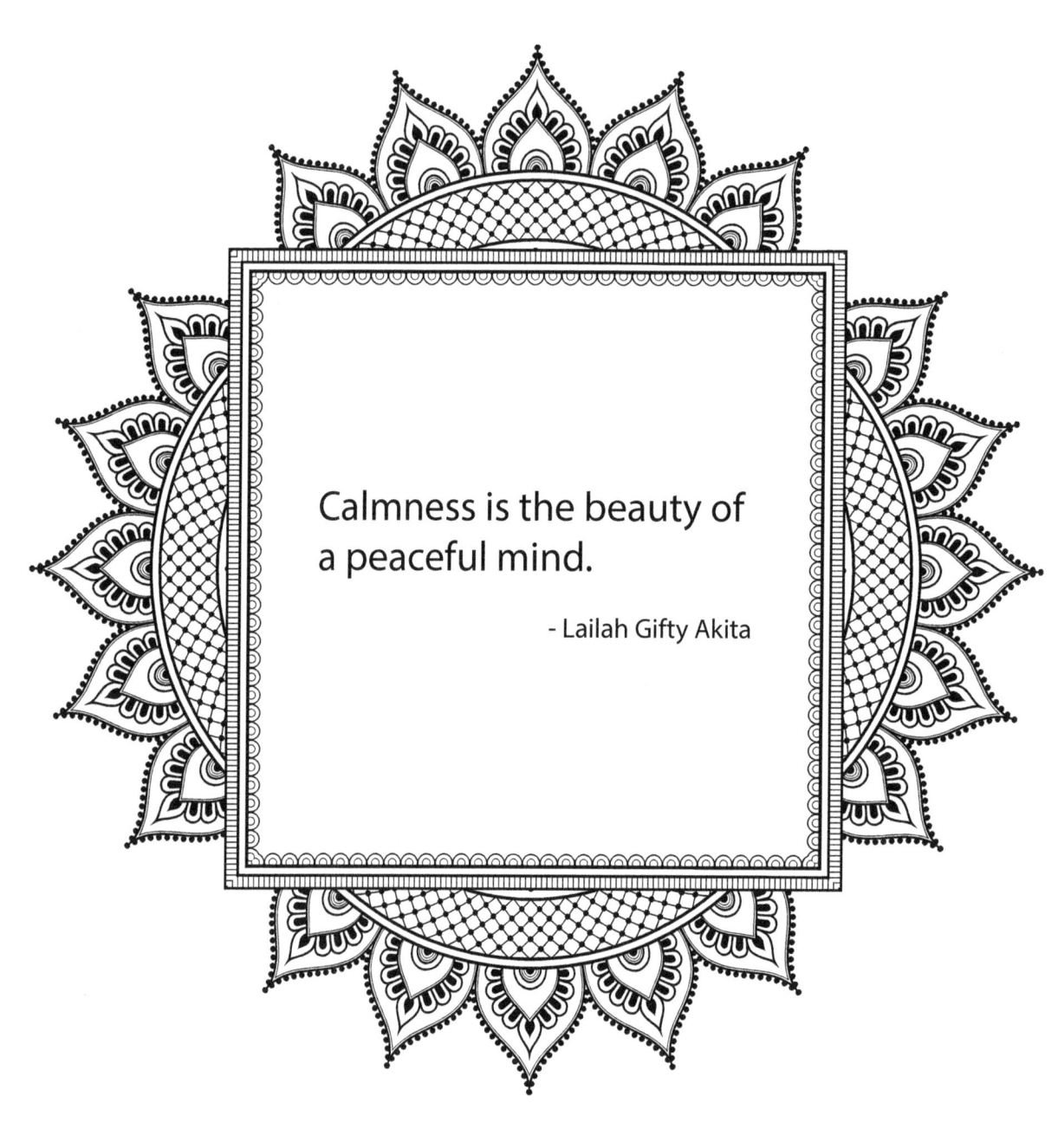

Calmness is the beauty of a peaceful mind.

- Lailah Gifty Akita

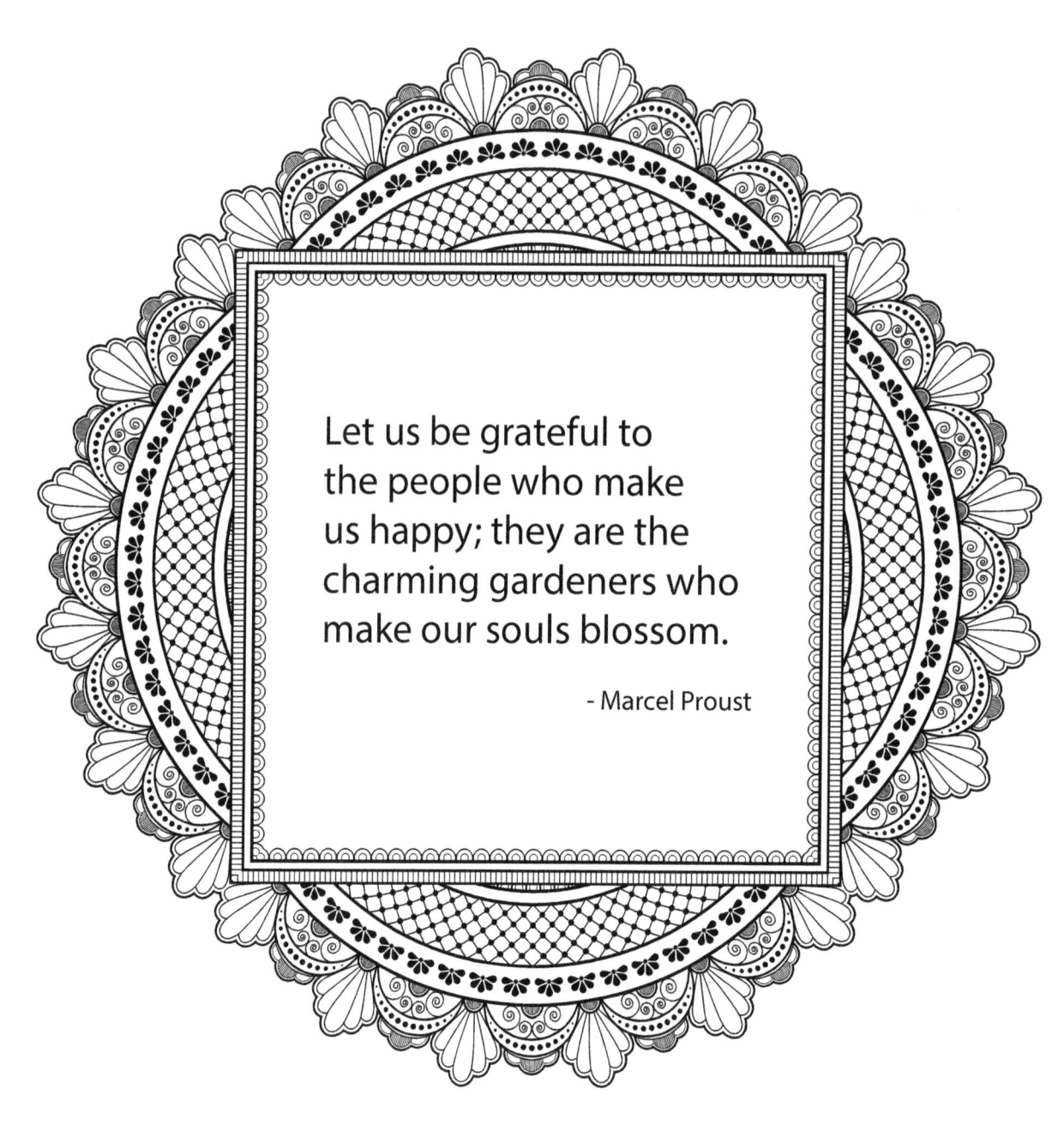

Let us be grateful to the people who make us happy; they are the charming gardeners who make our souls blossom.

- Marcel Proust

Life shrinks or expands in proportion to one's courage.

- Anaïs Nin

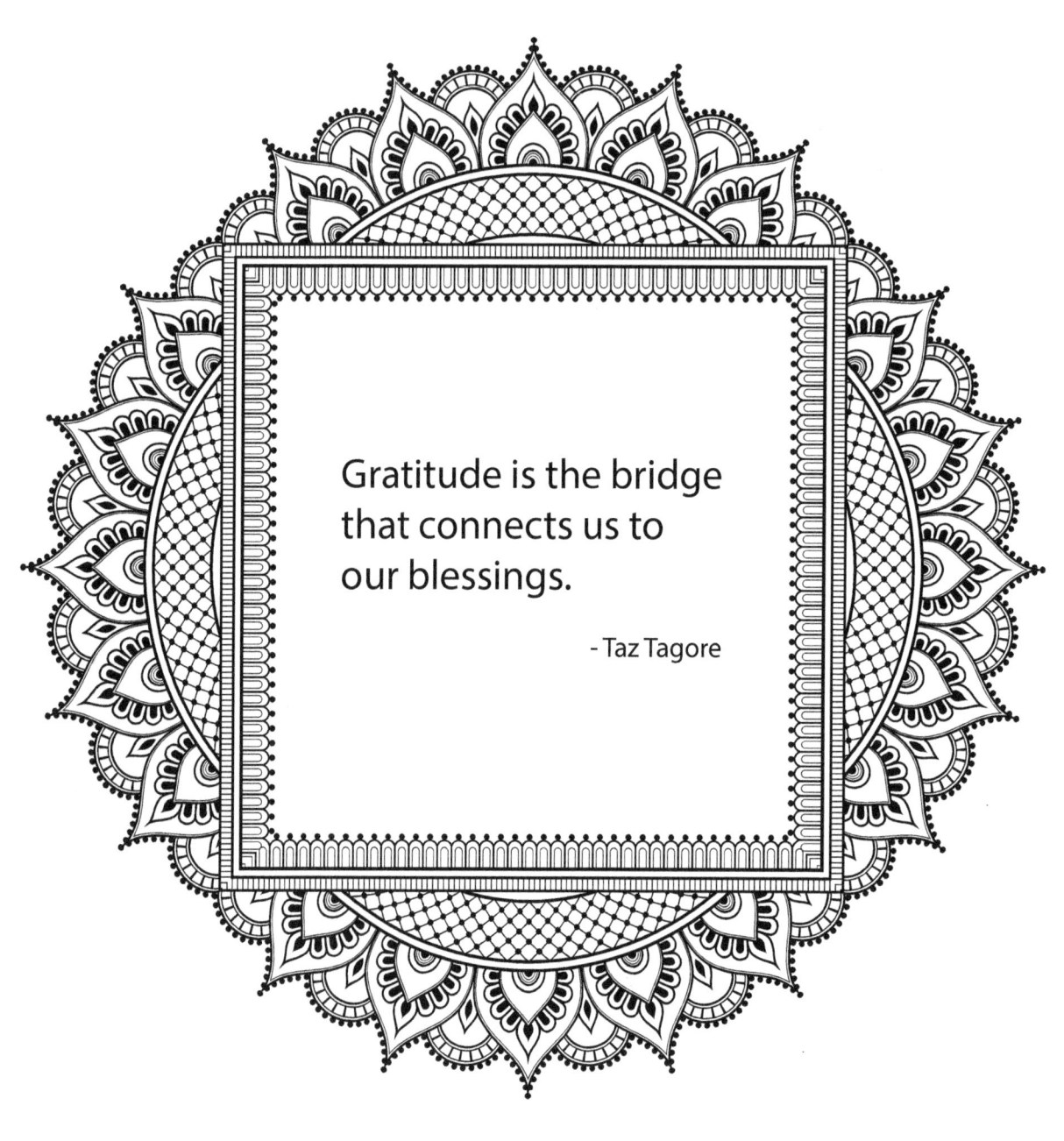

Gratitude is the bridge that connects us to our blessings.

- Taz Tagore

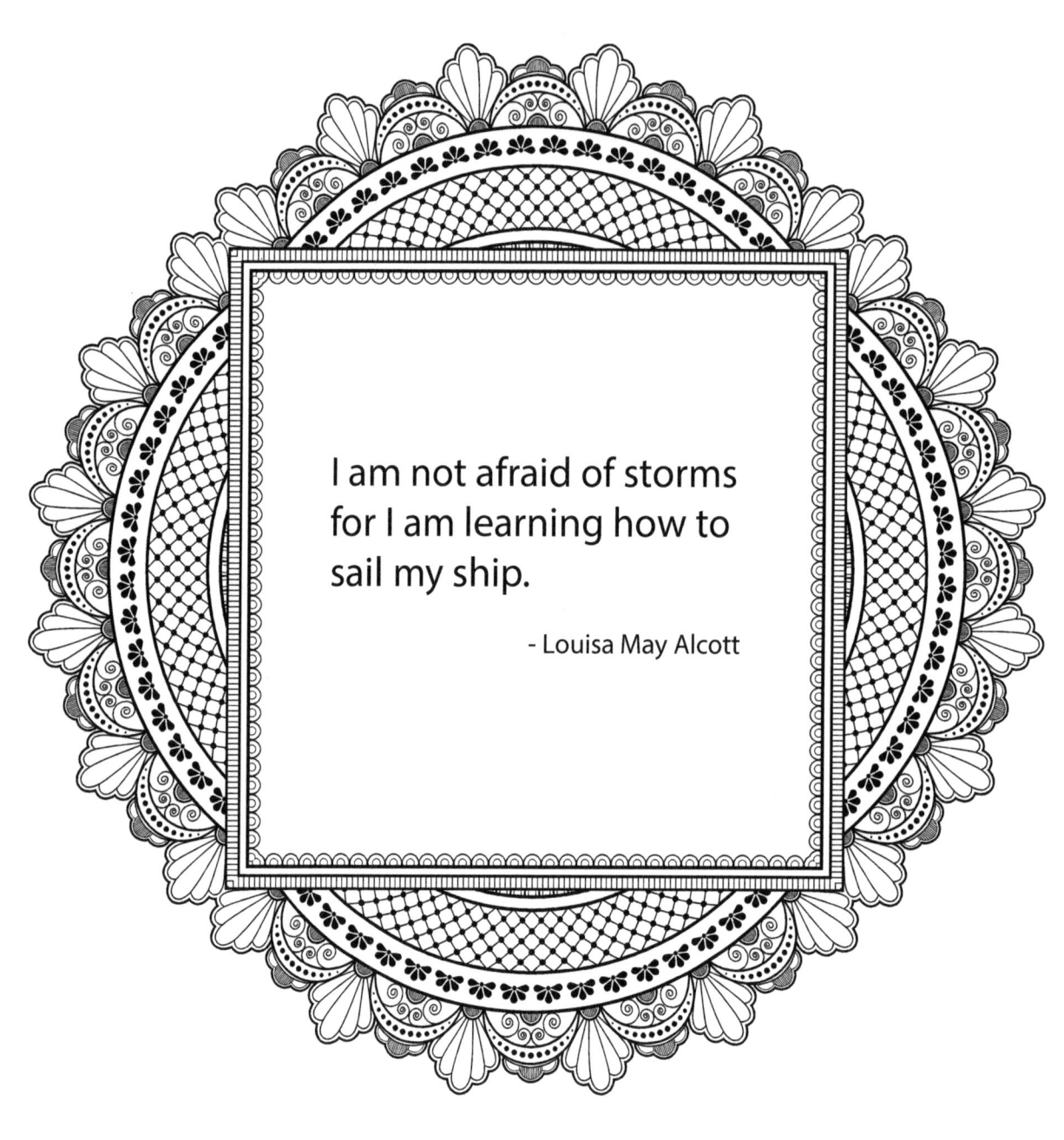

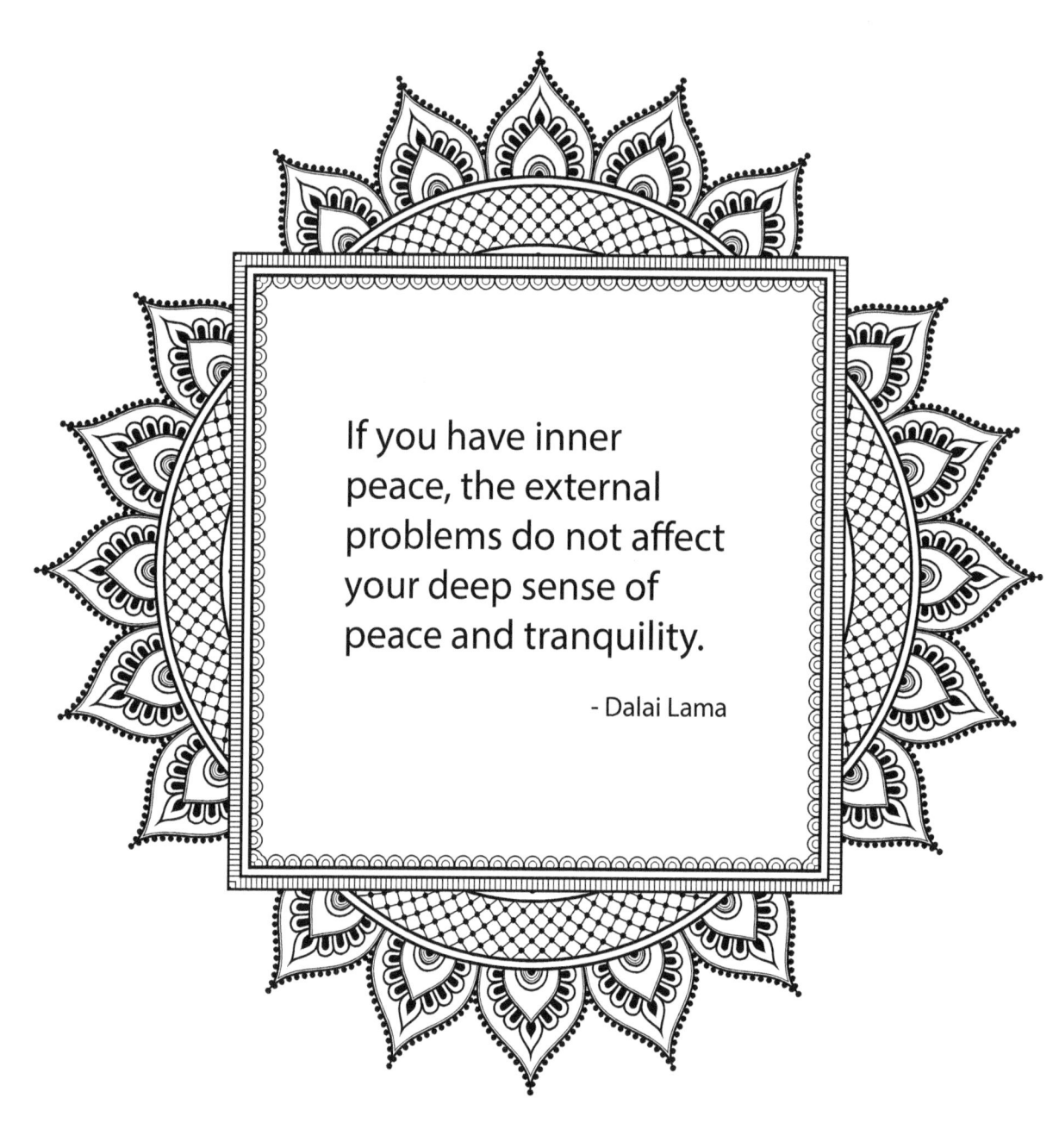

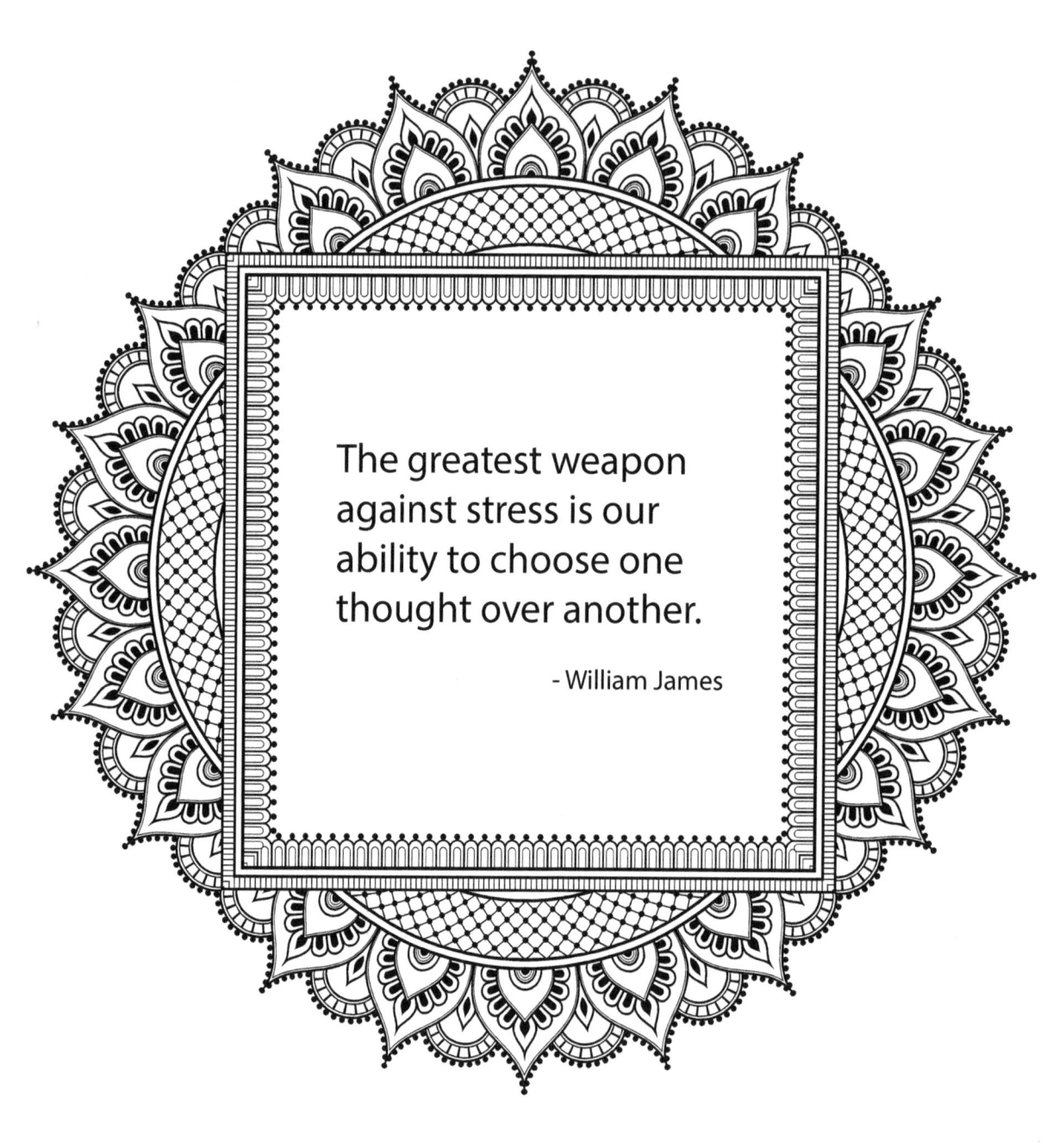

The greatest weapon against stress is our ability to choose one thought over another.

- William James

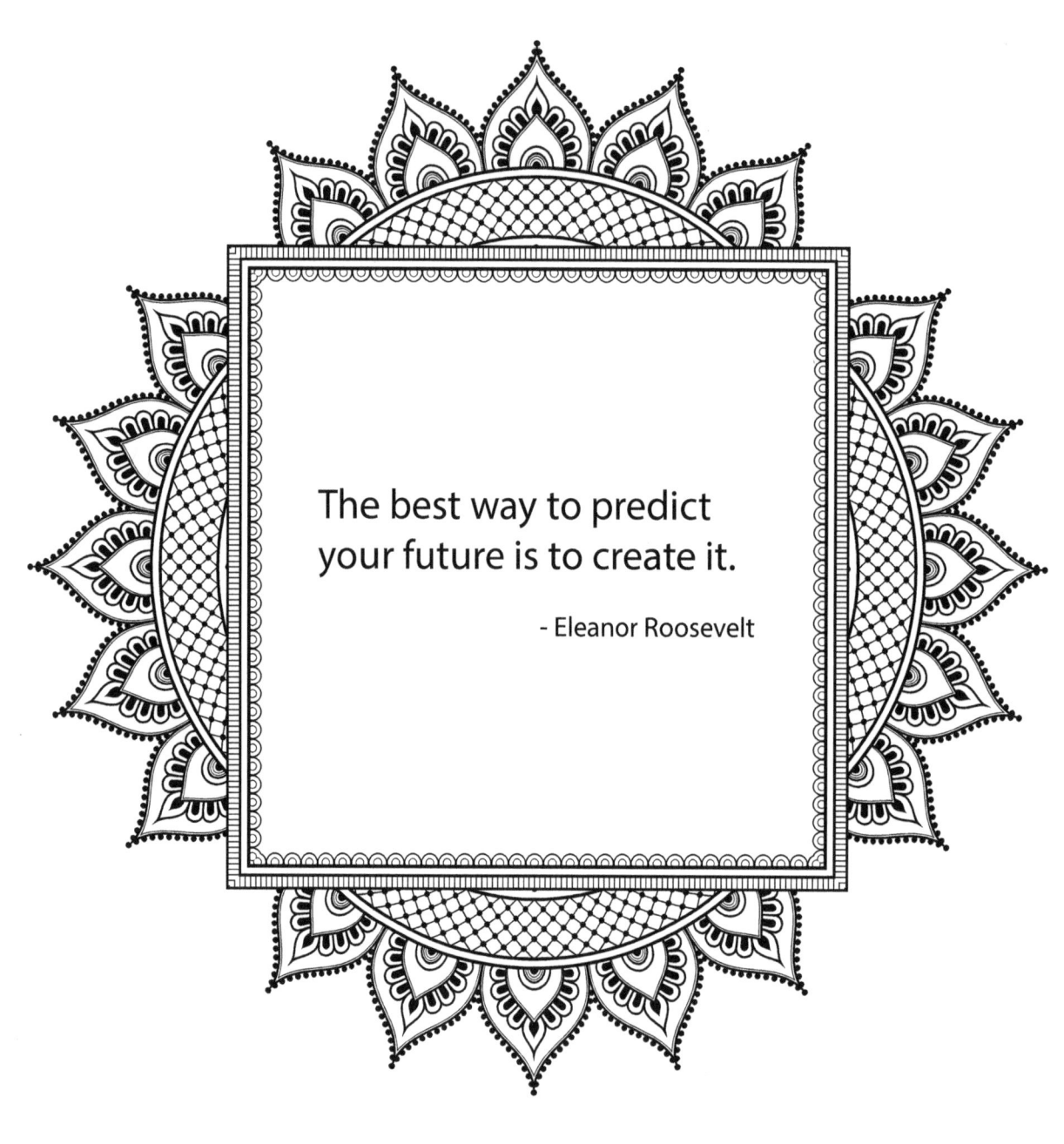

The best way to predict your future is to create it.

- Eleanor Roosevelt

www.ingramcontent.com/pod-product-compliance
Lightning Source LLC
Chambersburg PA
CBHW061121070526
44583CB00028B/3354